Table of Contents

Grade 6   Instructional Blackline Masters

Part 2: Writing, Listening, Speaking, and Viewing

Section 1: Expressing and Influencing

Section 2: Explaining and Informing

Section 3: Narrating and Entertaining

Using This Book

These blackline masters provide instructional support for lessons in *Houghton Mifflin English*, Grade 6. The following kinds of masters support lessons in the Getting Started, Grammar, and Writing units of the pupil book.

Getting Started: Listening, Speaking, and Viewing
- Listening and Speaking self-assessment checklist
- Viewing self-assessment checklist

Getting Started: The Writing Process
- Graphic organizer to support prewriting
- Writing conference support
- Revised/proofread working draft of the student model

Grammar Units (Units 1–7)
- Graphic organizers for summarizing grammar rules and concepts
- Sample responses for Writing Wrap-Up activities

Writing Units (Units 8–13)
- Revised working drafts of the student models
- Graphic organizers to support prewriting
- Writing evaluation checklists
- Writing conference support
- Sample form (Unit 11 only)
- Oral report rating sheet (Unit 11 only)

Most masters are grouped by unit and identified by a two-part label that represents the unit number and the sequence of the master within that unit. For example, 1–1 indicates the master is the first master for Unit 1. The numbers 9–6 indicate the page is the sixth master for Unit 9.

Masters for the opening Getting Started section are identified by the letters GS rather than a unit number. Grammar verses for all Grammar units are grouped together and labeled G.

Student writing models that span two or more pages have the same two-number label on each page plus the letter A, B, or C to indicate the sequence of pages for that model.

Each master is cross-referenced to the lesson(s) it supports. Similarly, lesson pages in the Teacher's Edition include cross-references to specific masters at point of use.

Name _____

Being a Good Listener and Speaker

Directions: Check the word you think best describes how you took part in the discussion.

When I Listened

1. I got rid of distractions so that I could hear. . . . . ☐ Yes ☐ No ☐ Partly
2. I didn't make distracting noises. . . . . ☐ Yes ☐ No ☐ Partly
3. I made eye contact with the speaker. . . . . ☐ Yes ☐ No ☐ Partly
4. I listened carefully and thought about what I heard. . . . . ☐ Yes ☐ No ☐ Partly
5. I asked questions about what I didn't understand. . . . . ☐ Yes ☐ No ☐ Partly
6. I silently summed up what was said. . . . . ☐ Yes ☐ No ☐ Partly

When I Spoke

1. I shared my ideas with the whole group. I didn't have side
   conversations. . . . . ☐ Yes ☐ No ☐ Partly
2. I made eye contact with my listeners. . . . . ☐ Yes ☐ No ☐ Partly
3. I spoke slowly, clearly, and loudly enough so that others could
   hear and understand me. . . . . ☐ Yes ☐ No ☐ Partly
4. I did not wander from the topic we discussed. . . . . ☐ Yes ☐ No ☐ Partly
5. I didn't interrupt others. . . . . ☐ Yes ☐ No ☐ Partly
6. I asked others what they thought of my ideas. . . . . ☐ Yes ☐ No ☐ Partly
7. I responded to the ideas of others. . . . . ☐ Yes ☐ No ☐ Partly
8. I was polite when I disagreed. . . . . ☐ Yes ☐ No ☐ Partly

Directions: Complete the sentences.

I believe I did a good job when I _____

_____.

I have difficulty when I speak, or listen, because _____

_____.

Next time I will _____

_____.

Name _____

Being a Good Viewer

Directions: Check the word you think best describes how viewing
helped you get information.

When I Viewed the World Around Me

1. I noticed all that I could to take in the "big picture." . . . . ☐ Yes   ☐ No   ☐ Partly

2. I noticed what attracted my attention. I thought about the most
   important part of what I was viewing. . . . . ☐ Yes   ☐ No   ☐ Partly

3. I focused more closely. I chose the important details of what I
   was viewing. . . . . ☐ Yes   ☐ No   ☐ Partly

When I Viewed Others

1. I paid attention to how people walked, stood, or sat. I watched
   body language to figure out what people might be saying without
   words. . . . . ☐ Yes   ☐ No   ☐ Partly

2. I noticed facial expressions and how faces expressed feelings. . . . . ☐ Yes   ☐ No   ☐ Partly

3. I looked at gestures. I watched how people used hand
   movements and head movements. I tried to figure out what
   these movements meant. . . . . ☐ Yes   ☐ No   ☐ Partly

When I Viewed a Still Image or Moving Images

1. I noticed where my eye was drawn when I looked at the image.
   I thought about the most important part of the image. . . . . ☐ Yes   ☐ No   ☐ Partly

2. I looked at the details in the image. . . . . ☐ Yes   ☐ No   ☐ Partly

3. I thought about why the image was made and who made it. . . . . . ☐ Yes   ☐ No   ☐ Partly

4. I thought about the audience for the image, and the message the
   image sent to that audience. . . . . ☐ Yes   ☐ No   ☐ Partly

5. I thought about how different audiences might respond to the
   image. . . . . ☐ Yes   ☐ No   ☐ Partly

6. I noticed the techniques that were used by the person or persons
   who made the image. . . . . ☐ Yes   ☐ No   ☐ Partly

7. I decided whether the image presented its subject in a fair or an
   unfair way. . . . . ☐ Yes   ☐ No   ☐ Partly

Name _____ **Directions:** Use this flow chart to help organize your information in chronological order.

Organizing a Description

First, group details by category. Then write the names of your categories in the boxes. Finally, list the details in each category. Put the groups of details in the order in which you plan to write about them.

1.

2.

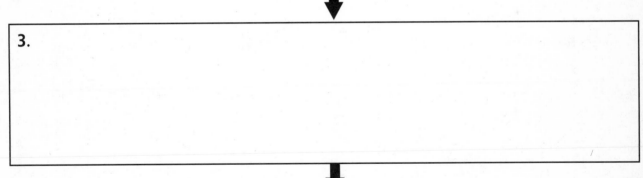

3.

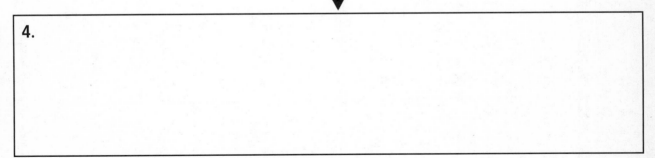

4.

Name _____

A Writing Conference
Description

Have a writing conference with a partner.

If you are the listener: Use the questions below to help you think about the description.

If you are the writer: Use the questions to help you think about what to ask your listener.

Questions for the Writing Conference

- What makes this topic good for a description?

- Does the beginning grab the reader's attention?

- Why do these details go together? Would organizing the details in a different way make the description easier to read?

- Were any parts hard to understand?

- Do all the details belong in this description?

- Does the ending share thoughts or feelings about the topic?

My Conference Notes

If you are the listener, make notes about what you like, what questions you have, or other suggestions. If you are the writer, make notes to remember your partner's thoughts or ideas of your own.

Here is James M. Glover's revised working draft of his description.

¶ Have you ever been in the woods after a rain? I went one late afternoon. The woods were an intense green, broccoli ~~The woods dripping trees looked like standing dollar bills.~~

~~Then I saw~~ as I walked, sopping wet leaves occasionally brushed my face and ~~dropped~~ splattered cold water on my hands. When the wind blew, it shook more water from the branches and rustled the leaves.

I thought I must be on a bridge with a clear stream trickling under me.

It kept rolling an acorn around in its tiny paws. Then scampered I saw only one animal, a furry gray squirrel. It ran up a tree

where it sat chattering at me.

As I walked on, I saw a line of light slanting through the tops of the trees like a

It was so bright and straight, I thought I could walk on it,

there were stairways of light everywhere. Then they stairway. After a few minutes ~~all the stairways of light~~ faded, and

I felt cold. It was getting late and time to go home.

Grammar Verse

Sentences

You can take a simple sentence,
Combine it with one more.
Use commas and conjunctions—
That's *and* or *but* or *or*.

Mixing simple and compound sentences,
You'll very quickly see
That your writing has more interest
When you add variety.

Use with Unit 1, The Sentence.

Grammar Verse

Nouns

Possessive nouns show ownership.
They do, they do.
Plurals stand for more than one—
At least, for two.

Both kinds of nouns may end with *s*.
Oho! Oho!
Possessives have an apostrophe,
But plurals? Oh, no!

Use with Unit 2, Nouns.

Grammar Verse

Verbs

Have you ever heard of
A transitive verb?
With a direct object
This verb is superb.

It transfers the action
From subject on down
To a word in the predicate—
A noun or pronoun.

Use with Unit 3, Verbs.

Grammar Verse

Adverbs

Adverbs are words with many uses.
This is what they do:
They modify other adverbs,
Verbs, and adjectives too.

Adverbs answer these three questions:
Where? or When? or How?
Some adverbs have an *ly* ending.
Some are like *there* or *now*.

Use with Unit 4, Modifiers.

Grammar Verse

Capitalization and Punctuation

Interjections can express what you feel:
Sadness, surprise—a happy squeal.
Hey, What, or *Bravo,*
Gee, Well, or *Oh,*
All right, or *Get real!*

Sometimes interjections stand alone.
They get punctuation of their own.
Say *Pow* (exclamation point!)
Ugh (exclamation point!)
In a forceful tone.

Use with Unit 5, Capitalization and Punctuation.

Grammar Verse

Pronouns

A pronoun that follows a linking verb
Takes the place of a predicate noun.
Look at it, though: it refers to the subject,
So write down a subject pronoun.

The noun in the subject is the antecedent
Of *I, you, it, she, he, they,* or *we.*
To check out your pronoun, reverse your sentence.
If it sounds right, you're as correct can be.

Use with Unit 6, Pronouns.

Grammar Verse

Prepositional Phrases

How do you make a prepositional phrase?
You take a preposition, such as *down* or *of* or *to.*
You add a noun or object pronoun,
And modifiers 'tween the two.

How do you use a prepositional phrase?
You use it as an adjective: Tell Which one? What kind?
You use it as an adverb: Tell How? When? Where?
Just keep those points in mind.

Use with Unit 7, Prepositional Phrases.

Directions: Complete each definition. Then write an example of each kind of sentence.

Definition: _____

The Sentence

Declarative

A declarative sentence is _____

End mark _____

Example _____

Interrogative

An interrogative sentence is _____

End mark _____

Example _____

Imperative

An imperative sentence is _____

End mark _____

Example _____

Exclamatory

An exclamatory sentence is _____

End mark _____

Example _____

Name _____

Subjects and Predicates

Definitions of Parts of a Sentence

Complete Subject:
Complete Predicate:
Simple Subject:
Simple Predicate:

A Sentence

_____

_____

Complete Subject

_____

_____

Complete Predicate

_____

_____

Simple Subject

_____

_____

Simple Predicate

_____

_____

Directions: Complete the definitions. Then write some sentences of your own.

Imperatives and Interrogatives

An imperative sentence _____

An interrogative sentence _____

Rule The subject of an imperative sentence _____ sentence _____.

Rule You can find the subject of an interrogative sentence _____.

Sentence	Subject
Get the cat some food, please.	_____
Close the window.	_____

Sentence	Subject
Is the cat hungry?	_____
Why is the window open?	_____

Write your own sentences.

Imperative Sentences

1 _____.

2 _____.

Interrogative Sentences

1 _____.

2 _____.

Compound Subjects, Compound Predicates, Compound Sentences

1–4

Directions: Complete each definition in the chart. Then write a sentence of each type.

Definitions	
Compound Sentence:	
Simple Sentence:	
Compound Predicate:	
Compound Subject:	

Sentence with a Compound Subject

and, or, but

Simple Sentence

Compound Sentence

Sentence with a Compound Predicate

Name _____ **Directions:** Complete each definition. List at least eight subordinate conjunctions. Then use four of those conjunctions to write complex sentences.

Conjunctions and Complex Sentences

A subordinating conjunction is _____
_____
_____
_____ .

A complex sentence is _____
_____
_____
_____ .

Some Subordinating Conjunctions

_____ _____ _____ _____

_____ _____ _____ _____

_____ _____ _____ _____

Complex Sentences

1 _____

2 _____

3 _____

4 _____

Name _____

Directions: Complete the statements below. Then rewrite the fragments and run-on sentences to make correct sentences.

Fragments and Run-ons

A sentence fragment is _____.

It can be corrected by _____.

A run-on sentence is _____.

It can be corrected by _____.

Fragment Students in the sixth-grade class

What was added: _____

_____

Fragment earned money for a class trip.

What was added: _____

_____

Run-on Some students wanted to go to the museum some wanted to go on a hike.

_____

_____

Run-on The class decided to have a vote, we voted by secret ballot.

_____

_____

1–6

LESSON 1

Writing Wrap-Up: Skit

Time Travel Agent: Welcome to Vacations in the Past, young man. Now, just tell me which era you'd like to visit.

Keith: I've always wanted to be a knight during the Middle Ages. I think summer might be the best season.

Time Travel Agent: In that case, let me make a few suggestions about the equipment you should bring.

Keith: Won't everything be provided at the castle? After all, I'm going to be a noble.

Time Travel Agent: Yes, of course, but there are a few modern conveniences that medieval castles lack. For example, you'll need some rash powder and flea spray. Suits of armor cause terrible heat rashes, you know, and I'm afraid that castle beds are simply swarming with fleas.

Keith: Oh no. I can't spend my vacation all itchy and flea-bitten! Send me back to last February when my parents took me to that luxury hotel in Bermuda.

LESSON 2

Writing Wrap-Up: Journal Entry

May 5

My family and I went to a Cinco de Mayo celebration this evening. Brightly dressed people were crowded together along the San Antonio Riverwalk. Venders sold tacos and tortillas. When the fireworks began, the river sparkled with color. A mariachi band played such lively tunes that everyone, even strangers, danced together.

LESSON 3

Writing Wrap-Up: Editorial

Which do you like better—riding on a bicycle or in a car? Your answer will probably depend on the kind of trip you want to take. Bicycles are great for short trips in the country. You can work up a sweat climbing a mountain and cool off as you coast down it. You can breathe the fresh air. You can explore narrow paths. Cars are better for bad weather or long trips on highways. They get you to your destination quickly. They shelter you from rain and cold. So take a bicycle when the trip is more important than the destination and a car when the destination is more important than the trip.

LESSON 4

Writing Wrap-Up: Safety Tips

Checklist for Bicycle Riders

Before you begin your ride, ask yourself these questions.
1. Is my head protected?
2. Do I have a safety reflector?

Once you are on the road, follow these rules.
1. Bike with the flow of traffic.
2. Keep a safe distance from parked cars.

LESSON 2

Writing Wrap-Up: Public Service Announcement

Lakes and oceans are being polluted. So students and volunteers must be recruited. Your clean-ups and protests can help preserve the natural beauty of our wildlife reserves. If you don't act now, priceless habitats will pass away. Join the Environmentalists Club today.

LESSON 6

Writing Wrap-Up: Flyer

Come and see the sixth grade soccer championships this Saturday! The sixth grade girls of Saratoga have trained and played with passion all season. Now they need your support for the most important game of the year. The game will be held at the Saratoga Soccer Center and is open to the community. Our cheerleaders will serve free food and perform a dance at halftime. So come and cheer your Saratoga soccer team on to victory!

LESSON 7

Writing Wrap-Up: Travel Brochure

Hull Beach is very peaceful, yet it is bursting with life. Brightly colored shells house delicate mollusks. The knotted cypress trees that hang over the cliffs flap and flutter with sea birds. The ocean reflects the sky, and its color is always changing. Dark green water lightens to gray blue. First the sunlight slicks the waves smooth, and then the wind whips them into foam. Children swim in the warm water, and grown-ups sunbathe on the sand. Some people visit Hull Beach for rest, some come for exercise, but everyone enjoys its beauty.

LESSON 8

Writing Wrap-Up: Weather Report

Today will be perfect for both sun worshipers and rain lovers. Sunshine and temperatures in the eighties will brighten the early part of the day, but light showers and temperatures in the sixties will cool the afternoon. By late evening, a thick fog will roll in and blanket the city. So prepare for variety. Wear light clothes to work and bring an umbrella for the walk home.

LESSON 10

Writing Wrap-Up: Letter

Dear Guidance Counselor,

I have so many interests that it's hard to settle for just one career. I can't decide whether I want to be a lawyer, a baseball player, a doctor, or a movie actor. My father is a lawyer. So, of course, he wants me to be one too. He can't talk too much about his clients because it's illegal. I can tell he really likes helping them, though. My mom says that I love to argue so much that I must be a born lawyer. It's true that I like to win arguments. I think that I might follow in my father's footsteps. It would make me feel really good to help people.

LESSON 9

Writing Wrap-Up: Speech

If you're like most people, you're probably afraid of spiders. I don't blame you. They are scary looking, and they have really bad reputations. If you knew the truth about them, though, you might have different feelings. A few species of spiders are deadly, but most are harmless. Spiders are useful because many species eat insects. So tell your mom not to sweep those webs away! Speaking of webs, scientists are trying to learn how to make artificial versions of the threads from which they are woven. Although they look delicate, these threads are stronger than any human-made fiber.

Next time you hear someone bad-mouthing spiders, tell him or her that, if there were a Most Valuable Species prize, spiders might win.

Name _____

Common and Proper Nouns

Directions: Complete the graphic organizer by writing the definitions. Then write some examples of your own.

Nouns

Definition: _____

Common Nouns

Definition: _____

Examples

Proper Nouns

Definition: _____

Examples

Name _____

Directions: Write singular nouns in the column on the left. Then write the other forms of those nouns in the three other columns. Include some nouns in your examples that do not follow the regular rules.

Singular and Plural Nouns, Possessive Nouns

Singular Noun	Plural Form	Singular Possessive	Plural Possessive

LESSON 1

Writing Wrap-Up: Press Release

Pioneer Technology is introducing a startling new alarm clock. What, you may ask, is so startling about a plain old alarm clock? Well, it's not its reliability. Many of our competitors turn out reliable clocks. It is startling precisely because it isn't startling! Our new Lark alarm will coax you awake every morning with your favorite song. You can even program it to wake you with a poem or a cheerful greeting. So buy a Lark alarm clock and start every day with a song and a smile.

LESSON 2

2–3

Writing Wrap-Up: Review

The new sitcom, Baseball Blues, aired its pilot episode on WBVH, Channel 12, last Friday night. The star, Mark Mathews, is a pitcher who has difficulty finding the plate. On the first Saturday of the season, Mark has difficulty even finding the game! The Knights' catcher gets lost in Brooklyn, and a mysterious Peruvian shows up in his place. A right fielder named Ray believes every baseball has a personality and some should be set free rather than caught. Baseball Blues is a very funny and smart comedy about American sports. Even with the Knights' batting average below 200, Baseball Blues should be the smash hit of the millennium!

LESSON 3

Writing Wrap-Up: Poem

One warm, quiet evening we took a pizza to the park.
We sat beneath the trees watching
Squirrels search for acorns in the dusk.

Slowly we ate our pizza, listening to the soft sounds
Of crickets chirping, leaves rustling, trees sighing
in the wind.

LESSON 4

Writing Wrap-Up: Encyclopedia Article

John Fitzgerald Kennedy, Joseph Kennedy's second
son, became America's youngest president in 1961.
His term in office was cut short by an assassin's bullet,
but his spirit continues to influence American politics.
He won a Navy Corps Medal for his courageous service
in World War II. Perhaps Kennedy's greatest attribute
as a leader was his ability to inspire others. He gave us
a new vision of America's future, uniting us in a
common cause.

LESSON 5

Writing Wrap-Up: Tongue Twisters

Please paste posters on Pizzi Plaza's plaster pillars.
Basking asps in drafts hiss raspingly at last.
Sidney snatched the snickering snackers' sneakers.

Name _____

Action Verbs and Direct Objects

Action Verb

An action verb tells _____
_____.

Sentence _____
_____

Action verb _____

Verb Phrase

A verb phrase is _____
_____.

Sentence _____
_____

Main verb _____   **Helping verb** _____

Direct Object

Definition: _____
_____

Sentence _____
_____

Direct object _____

Directions: Complete the definitions. Then choose two verbs from the box. Make each verb transitive in one sentence and intransitive in another sentence.

Transitive and Intransitive Verbs

Verbs		
look	sing	paint
remember	walk	listen

Transitive Verbs

A transitive verb is _____

Sentences

1 _____

2 _____

Intransitive Verbs

An intransitive verb is _____

Sentences

1 _____

2 _____

3-2

Name _____

Directions: Complete the definitions. Then write sample sentences.

Being and Linking Verbs

Being Verbs

A being verb is _____
_____ .

Linking Verbs

A linking verb is _____
_____ .

Predicate Noun

Definition: _____

Sentences

1 _____

2 _____

Predicate Adjective

Definition: _____

Sentences

1 _____

2 _____

Name _____ **Directions:** Fill in the definitions and write example sentences in the first two charts. Then complete the chart at the bottom of the page.

Tenses

Present	Past	Future
Definition: _____ _____	Definition: _____ _____	Definition: _____ _____
Sentence _____ _____ _____	Sentence _____ _____ _____	Sentence _____ _____ _____

Perfect Tenses

Present Perfect	Past Perfect	Future Perfect
Definition: _____ _____	Definition: _____ _____	Definition: _____ _____
Sentence _____ _____ _____	Sentence _____ _____ _____	Sentence _____ _____ _____

Irregular Verbs

Verb	Present Participle	Past	Past Participle
	(is) being		
		did	
			(has) driven
speak			
		wrote	

Name _____

Directions: Write the rules. Then write example sentences. In the last chart give the correct form of the verb and write a sample sentence.

3–5

Subject-Verb Agreement

With Singular Subject

Rule _____
_____

Example _____
_____

With Plural Subject

Rule _____
_____

Example _____
_____

Compound Subjects

With *and*

Rule _____
_____

Example _____
_____

With *or, either…or, neither…nor*

Rule _____
_____

Example _____
_____

Starting with *here* or *there*

Rule _____
Example _____

Agreement with the Verb *be*

Subject	Present	Past
I	_____	_____
he, she, it, and all singular nouns	_____	_____
we, you, they, and all plural nouns	_____	_____

Name _____

Directions: Write the definition and the rule. Then fill in the charts.

Contractions

Definition: _____

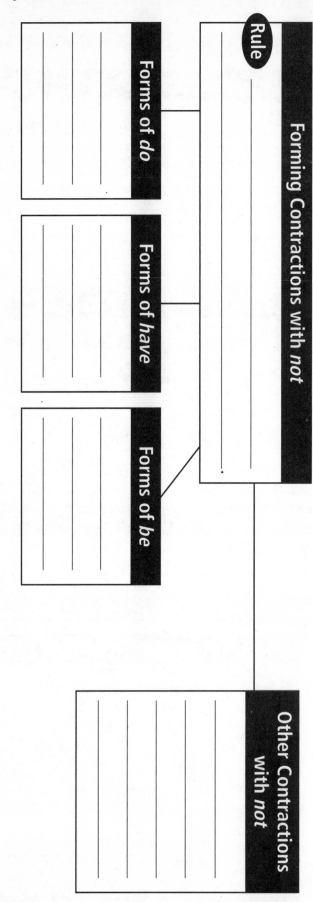

Forming Contractions with *not*

Rule _____

Forms of *do*

Forms of *have*

Forms of *be*

Other Contractions with *not*

Name _____   **Directions:** Write the correct words. Then
                                    write sample sentences.

teach/learn

To get instruction _____

To give instruction _____

Sentences

_____

_____

_____

_____

sit/set

To rest upright _____

To place an object _____

Sentences

_____

_____

_____

_____

lie/lay

To rest or recline _____

To place an object _____

Sentences

_____

_____

_____

_____

Verb Usage

let/leave

To go away _____

To permit _____

Sentences

_____

_____

_____

_____

rise/raise

To get up or go up _____

To move something up _____

Sentences

_____

_____

_____

_____

lend/borrow

To take temporarily _____

To give temporarily _____

Sentences

_____

_____

_____

_____

LESSON 1

Writing Wrap-Up: Report Notes

- Dolphins swim up to thirty miles per hour.
- Like whales, they breathe through a blowhole at the top of their back.
- Dolphins make high-pitched noises through their blowholes.
- People often confuse dolphins with porpoises.
- Fishermen sometimes accidentally trap dolphins in tuna nets.

LESSON 2

Writing Wrap-Up: Press Release

Albert Einstein has always been a star in the scientific world. Now he will star in DBC's new cartoon series, The Mad Scientist. You will laugh at Einstein's absent-minded mistakes and marvel at his dramatic discoveries. The show makes science come alive. Einstein's ideas about time and space will change how you see the world. You should tune into Channel 12 at 9:00 A.M. this Saturday to see not only a new cartoon but also a whole new universe.

LESSON 3

Writing Wrap-Up: Clues to "Guess Who"

Guess Who

- I split rails and clerked in a store when I was young.
- I practiced law in Springfield, Illinois.
- I won the presidential election in 1860.
- I fought the Civil War to keep the United States one nation.
- I opposed slavery and issued the Emancipation Proclamation on January 1, 1863.

LESSON 4

Writing Wrap-Up: Jokes

What animal can tell the time?
Answer: A watchdog

What animal is an escape artist?
Answer: A flea

What fruit is two in one?
Answer: A pear

LESSON 5

Writing Wrap-Up: Editorial

At my elementary school, athletes, musicians, and scholars all seem to stick together in special groups, or cliques. The advantage of cliques is the bond of friendship they create. This bond makes the group members feel included and important. The disadvantage of cliques is that they make nonmembers feel left out. I would like to remind clique members that leaving others out is not a good way to feel proud of yourself.

Unit 3 Verbs

LESSON 6

Writing Wrap-Up: Headlines

President Will Oppose Tax Cuts

Nolan Ryan Voted into Hall of Fame

New Drug Will Help Stroke Victims

Shuttle Soars into Space

American Wins Tour de France

Unit 3 Verbs

LESSON 7

Writing Wrap-Up: Letter

Dear Raoul,

Remember when I used to dream of moving from Hilton? Well, now I miss it. I even miss cranky Mrs. Drake and the way she used to glare at me. (Man, you'd think I had committed every crime in the book.) The rest of my family loves this city! My parents have decided to be sophisticated. They're always running to art films, to openings (whatever they are), and to ethnic (?) restaurants. Before the end of this month, I'll bet Katie will have made more friends than she had at home. My dad says I haven't tried. What does he want? I've joined the swim team and computer club at school. But that hasn't helped. The kids had already formed their own little groups long before I showed up. Oh well, I'll keep trying. Who knows? By the time you get this letter, maybe I'll have gotten into the swing of things.

Your friend,

Brian

Unit 3 Verbs

LESSON 8

Writing Wrap-Up: Captions

John has stolen a chocolate chip cookie.

Sara has made her brother's blanket into a costume.

This group has been all the way up Mt. Everest.

Jorge has flown a kite.

LESSON 9

Writing Wrap-Up: Book Review

The Outsiders, by S. E. Hinton, is about growing up. Its hero, Ponyboy Curtis, has problems at home and in school. Ponyboy and his friends live in a rough neighborhood. They are in a gang called "The Greasers," a name given to them by a group of rich kids called "The Socs." Ponyboy thinks that he can't escape from gang life because he is so poor. He has no control over the tensions in his school and gang. How does Ponyboy learn to be his own person? Read The Outsiders to find out.

LESSON 10

Writing Wrap-Up: Essay

My family and I recently moved to a new house in the suburbs. Neither my younger sister, Jennifer, nor I expected the move to be such a dramatic change. Here we have to take the bus or drive to school. There we could walk when the weather was nice. Life is much quieter here. But sometimes I miss the noise of traffic and the crowds of people on the city streets. I especially miss the smell of hot pizza coming from Tony's Italian restaurant on the corner of my old block. I wish it were not necessary to choose either the city or the suburbs. Maybe someday we will find a neighborhood that combines the quiet of the suburbs with the smell of Tony's pizza.

LESSON 11

Writing Wrap-Up: Dialogue

Boris: Thomas! You'll never believe what I've just heard.

Thomas: You're right. I almost never do.

Boris: I'm serious! Do you remember what we did yesterday?

Thomas: How could I forget beating you fifteen times in a row in video basketball? I've never enjoyed myself more.

Boris: Well, if we hadn't been playing video games, we could've seen the Knicks' Play-Offs Parade. Professional basketball players actually walked right past our house!

Thomas: Now I'm depressed. There's only one thing to do about it.

Boris: What's that?

Thomas: We'll have to spend another whole day playing video basketball!

LESSON 12

Writing Wrap-Up: Instructions

Do not raise your puppy to bite the neighbors, even if they yell at you.

Do not let your puppy rise early and wake your parents, even if they make you go to bed too early.

Do not train your puppy to sit or lie down on your younger brother, even if he complains too much.

Do not set your puppy in a pool, even if he could use a good cleaning.

Do not lay your puppy on the kitchen table, even if you want to get out of eating your vegetables.

Unit 3   Verbs

LESSON 13

Writing Wrap-Up: Bulletin Board Notices

Join the Spanish Club! Learn to speak Spanish and dance salsa!

Do you ever leave your homework in your locker? Now you can learn everything you forgot to bring home by connecting to the new Internet site, homework.com.

Sign up for the Athletic Club! All you have to do is join. We lend members all necessary sports equipment for free!

What is the Mentor Program? It's a program dedicated to learning. You will teach younger, disadvantaged students, who, in turn, will teach you valuable lessons about courage and determination.

Don't let movie stars have all the fun! Be a part of the Drama Society and take center stage!

No More Renting! Borrow Our Computers at No Cost!

Unit 3   Verbs

Name _____

Directions: Complete the definition. Then give examples and write sentences for each type of adjective.

4–1

Adjectives

An adjective is _____

high	the	huge	several	beautiful	an	that	these
four	small	twenty-year-old	a	those	ninety	happy	this

What Kind?

Examples _____

Sentence _____

Which One?

Examples _____

Sentence _____

How Many?

Examples _____

Examples _____

Sentence _____

Articles

Examples _____

Sentence _____

Predicate Adjective

Examples _____

Sentence _____

4–2

Directions: Fill in the definitions and rules on each part of the graphic organizer. Give examples as asked.

Comparing with Adjectives

A comparative adjective compares _____.

A superlative adjective compares _____.

Spelling Changes in Comparative and Superlative Forms

Examples:

Adjective	Comparative	Superlative

Rule _____

Rule _____

Rule _____

Rule For longer words, _____

Name _____

Directions: Choose five proper nouns from Box A. Write proper adjectives formed from those nouns in Box C. Then choose a word from Box B and complete a phrase.

Proper Adjectives

Box A

China	Ireland
Italy	Europe
Japan	Russia
Canada	Africa

Box B

clothing	cars
vegetables	technology
pasta	food
songs	stories

Box C

_____

_____

_____

_____

_____

Use with Lesson 5.

Grade 6   Unit 4 Modifiers Blackline Master 4–3

Copyright © Houghton Mifflin Company. All rights reserved.

Name _____

Directions: Complete the definitions. Then give examples and write sentences for each type of adverb.

4—4

Adverbs

An adverb _____

How?

Examples _____

Sentence _____

When?

Examples _____

Sentence _____

Where?

Examples _____

Sentence _____

To What Extent?

Examples _____

Sentence _____

Negative

Examples _____

Sentence _____

Name _____

Directions: Write the comparative and the superlative forms of the adverbs listed in the center. Complete the rest of the Venn Diagram. Then choose one adverb and use its forms in a sentence.

4–5

Comparing with Adverbs

Comparative
The comparative form compares _____ things.

Rule _____

Most Adverbs _____

Examples _____
_____

Irregular Adverbs _____
_____
_____
_____
_____
_____

lightly
much
little
carefully
carelessly
fast
well

Superlative
The superlative form compares _____ things.

Rule _____

Most Adverbs _____

Examples _____
_____

Irregular Adverbs _____
_____
_____
_____
_____
_____

Sentence 1 (comparative form) _____
_____ .

Sentence 2 (superlative form) _____
_____ .

LESSON 1

Writing Wrap-Up: Ad

Are you too rushed to shower in the morning? Purchase an Insta-Shower at a Super Clean store near you and get ten more minutes of blissful sleep every morning. All you have to do is press the button on our pocket-sized personal hygiene computer, and your entire body will be cleaned by warm electronic waves.

LESSON 2

Writing Wrap-Up: Letter

Dear Bernice,

I'm glad you can visit. I'll show you my favorite places. One of these is Arrow Park. Remember that park where we used to ride our bikes? Well, this one is larger and has great bike paths. The best path leads to an old millpond. We can have a picnic there and feed the ducks and geese with the leftovers. Those geese can be fierce though. An angry one hissed at me last week. I'll never feed that one again.

Your friend,
Latisha

LESSON 3

Writing Wrap-Up: Almanac Facts

1. The secret to making good hot chocolate is combining the darkest chocolate with the creamiest milk.

2. Flying to school in a hot air balloon is slower than taking the bus.

3. The longest distance I have ever swum is two miles.

4. The highest hill in my town is located behind the high school.

5. Carol is a better dancer than Brenda, but Brenda has a sweeter voice.

6. Jason's dog is smellier than mine.

7. Kyle holds the neighborhood record for telling the wildest tall tales.

8. Mr. Atkins is the teacher with the loudest voice.

9. The strawberries in Gloria's garden are juicier than the ones in mine.

10. Jeremy won the prize for being the funniest boy in class.

LESSON 4

Writing Wrap-Up: Questions

1. Which city has more people—Berlin or Beijing?
2. Which state has less water—Arizona or New Mexico?
3. Who is more famous—Babe Ruth or Hercules?
4. Which country has the least rainfall?
5. Who has the most powerful backhand in tennis?

Unit 4   Modifiers

LESSON 6

Writing Wrap-Up: How To

Raising chickens is a process that never really ends. Gently place newly laid eggs in a warm incubator. You should turn them carefully every day, like a real mother hen caring for her young. After almost a month, the chicks will crack open their egg from the inside, and you can see them wobble eagerly into the world. Their skinny legs can barely hold them up. Over the next six weeks, the chicks grow very rapidly. They spend a lot of time with their friends clucking loudly. Then the process begins all over again, as the baby chicks gradually become hens and lay their own eggs.

Unit 4   Modifiers

LESSON 5

Writing Wrap-Up: Recipe

International Gumbo

3 cups finely chopped Spanish onions
1 cup finely chopped garlic
1 tablespoon Italian olive oil
1 tablespoon Malaysian peanut oil
1 16-ounce can tomatoes
1 cup diced American ham
4 quarts Israeli chicken stock
3 cups Japanese rice
1 cup grated English cheddar cheese
2 tablespoons flour

Now you can combine ingredients from the far corners of the world into a simple, delicious International Gumbo. Sauté the onions and garlic in the olive oil. In another frying pan, brown the flour in the peanut oil. Combine the sautéed onions and garlic and the browned flour in a large pot. Add the ham and tomatoes, and cook for 10 minutes. Then add the rice and pour in the chicken stock. Let your gumbo simmer for 1 hour. Sprinkle with the grated cheddar cheese before serving.

Unit 4   Modifiers

4-7

LESSON 7

Writing Wrap-Up: Captions

My brother is smiling very proudly upon his graduation from Penn State. He was the first person in our family to receive a college degree.

Our family seems absolutely relaxed and happy on our day at the beach. On day-trips like this, our whole family comes together.

Adam looks so funny here! He was dressed as a rock star for the school's pep rally.

Unit 4   Modifiers

LESSON 8

Writing Wrap-Up: Character Sketch

My friend Jennifer tells stories more dramatically than anyone else in my class does. She is best at making up imaginary tales. She tells almost as much with her facial expressions and with her gestures as she does with her voice. She can roll her eyes more comically and squint more wickedly than anyone I have ever known. The movements of her hands are more graceful than some dancers' are. I like Jennifer's stories better than the stories I see on TV because she puts so much of herself in them.

Unit 4   Modifiers

LESSON 9

Writing Wrap-Up: Interview

- Is it true that after the American Revolution, Britain's place in world politics was never the same?
- Didn't any of the American colonists remain loyal to Britain?
- Is it true that before the Revolution, the colonists couldn't elect their own leaders?
- Why did the Americans throw shiploads of tea into Boston Harbor? Didn't they like English tea?
- Why couldn't the Americans have become independent peacefully?

Unit 4   Modifiers

LESSON 10

Writing Wrap-Up: Letter

Dear Editor,

In 1951, when Martin Luther King Jr. was in college, African Americans were treated badly. They could not even sit with whites in the front of a bus. Ten years later, African Americans were sharing more than the front of the bus with whites. They were sharing restaurants, schools, jobs, and swimming pools. King's great courage was behind many of these changes. He fought to end the bad treatment of African Americans, but he fought with ideas, not violence. He spoke so well that whites and African Americans joined together around a common cause—justice. A true hero is a person like Martin Luther King Jr., who fights courageously for a good cause, even when the fight is very difficult.

Sincerely,
Kerrie Hon

Unit 4   Modifiers

4-9

Name _____

Directions: Complete each definition. Show correct punctuation.
Then write an example of each type of sentence.

Reviewing End Punctuation

Type of Sentence	Punctuation	Example
Declarative Definition: _____		
Imperative Definition: _____		
Interrogative Definition: _____		
Exclamatory Definition: _____		

5-1

5-2

Directions: Complete the definitions. Write examples of proper nouns and proper adjectives. Then complete the definitions and the rules for interjections. Write sentences that include interjections.

Proper Nouns

A proper noun is _____ .

People	Places	Things	Days, Months, Holidays
___	___	___	___
___	___	___	___
___	___	___	___
___	___	___	___

Proper Adjectives

A proper adjective is _____ .

Examples

_____
_____
_____
_____
_____

Interjections

An interjection is _____ .

Rule If it stands alone, it ends _____ .

Rule If it begins a sentence, it is set off by _____ .

Sentence 1 _____ .

Sentence 2 _____ .

Name _____

Directions: Write the rule and an example sentence in each box.

5–3

Commas

With Words in a Series

Rule _____

Example _____

With Appositives

Rule _____

Example _____

With Introductory Words

Rule _____

Example _____

With Direct Address

Rule _____

Example _____

Name _____ **Directions:** Complete the abbreviations in the chart. Then complete the rules about titles, and write an example for each.

Abbreviations and Titles

Word	Abbreviation
Street	_____
Mountain	_____
Post Office	_____
Company	_____
inch	_____
miles per hour	_____
Apartment	_____

Type of Work	How to Mark	Example
book	_____	_____
magazine	_____	_____
song	_____	_____
movie	_____	_____

Name _____ **Directions:** Write the rules and a sample
sentence for each box. Use correct
capitalization and punctuation.

When Speaker's Name Precedes the Dialogue

Rules _____

_____

_____

Sentence _____

_____

_____

When Speaker's Name Follows the Dialogue

Rules _____

_____

_____

Sentence _____

_____

_____

Punctuating Dialogue

When Speaker's Name Interrupts the Dialogue

Rules _____

_____

Sentence _____

_____

LESSON 1

Writing Wrap-Up: TV Script

Are you ready to rock and roll? Today I will show you how to howl like a punk rock star, how to shake the sky with a scream. The secret is energy! Reach way down into your belly. Gather your strength, your feelings, and all of the hidden shouts that have no way out in your everyday life. Then let them go in a natural, deep release —LIKE THIS! Now, are you ready to try it on your own? Just make sure that you actually are on your own, not in a crowded place, like a classroom!

Unit 5 **Capitalization and Punctuation**

LESSON 2

Writing Wrap-Up: Editorial

The Bard Community Park is in danger, but if we act now, it can still be saved. Last night, the Sequoia City Council voted to have the park torn down and a new highway constructed in its place. I think we have all spent sunny Saturdays playing Little League Baseball in the fields there or quiet Sundays relaxing in the grass. Remember the importance and beauty of the park. Come join demonstrators at City Hall on Thursday at 3:15 P.M., and show your support for Bard Community Park.

Unit 5 **Capitalization and Punctuation**

LESSON 3

Writing Wrap-Up: Letter

Hi, Garrison!

I saw that new comedy *Ain't We Got Fun?* Wow! It's so funny. It's about two old friends who stick together even in hard times. In one scene, they get caught in a store robbery and become friends with the robber by showing him their collection of baseball cards. It's all they've got in their wallets. All right. I won't ruin the movie by telling you the entire story. Hey, remember *Season's Greetings*, the comedy we saw last winter? Well, *Ain't We Got Fun?* is even funnier! So do yourself a favor and see it. Write soon and let me know what you think.

Your buddy,

Davis

Unit 5 **Capitalization and Punctuation**

LESSON 4

Writing Wrap-Up: Personal Inventory

- If I had to spend a week alone on a desert island, I would bring good books, my favorite music, and a truck full of ice cream.
- I spend my weekends seeing friends, watching movies, and exploring the city.
- My favorite foods are pizza, barbecued chicken, and cheesecake.
- I would like to learn many different languages, travel the world, and make good friends along the way.
- I may become a lawyer, a scientist, or a professional football player.
- During lunch break, I eat lunch, talk to my friends, and rest in the park.

Unit 5 Capitalization and Punctuation

LESSON 6

Writing Wrap-Up: Classified Ad

Free Kittens! Four beautiful kittens now need homes. They come from a loving and lovable mother, and a long line of adorable cats. Their best quality—cuddliness! Hurry up and adopt one before we become too attached. The address is 2013 Church Street, Montrose, Colorado. Ask for Mister Bookman, Doctor Bookman, or Mary. You will be greeted with a smile and a purr.

Unit 5 Capitalization and Punctuation

LESSON 5

Writing Wrap-Up: Interview

Question: Today I am going to interview myself, because there are no other interviewers who can speak fluent Antlish, fit into my ant-hole, or hear my ant-voice. In addition, the professional interviewers I contacted at ABD brutally attempted to step on me. So, Mr. Ant, how do you spend most of your time?

Answer: Well, that's a very interesting, engaging, and thoughtful question. Almost every day is different for me. Usually I spend my time going to picnics, constructing majestic anthills, and sneaking into human kitchens.

Question: Can you tell me about your hopes for the future?

Answer: Well, sure, I have my hopes and dreams just like any other ant. Someday I'd like to settle down, build a nice hill, and raise an enormous colony. But I guess for now, I am happy roaming the world.

Unit 5 Capitalization and Punctuation

LESSON 7

Writing Wrap-Up: Dialogue

"You know, you really shouldn't eat so much candy," said Ben.

"Yeah," Adam replied. "But I really love it."

"Well," Ben said with a chuckle, "your teeth don't really love it and neither does the rest of your body. Haven't you ever noticed how wired you feel after eating candy?"

Adam sighed. "Has my mom been talking to you? I've heard all that before. Haven't you ever heard of fluoride? Give me one really good reason not to eat candy."

"Okay," Ben said, as he reached into a bakery box. "You shouldn't eat so much candy so you'll have room for cake. Now, do you want some of this?" he asked, passing Adam a slice of chocolate fudge cake.

Unit 5   Capitalization and Punctuation

LESSON 8

Writing Wrap-Up: Calendar of Events

9/1   Actor Matt Connory will speak about his new movie, Dance of the Leprechaun, and then recite Irish poetry in his famous brogue.

9/7   Julia Thomas discusses her new cookbook, Eating for Pleasure, and offers a free full-course meal for all students in attendance.

9/19   New York News editor, Ron Garren, reads Baseball with Henny Youngman, a chapter from his new, best-selling book, Celebrity Sports Celebration.

9/26   The Rice Girls dance their world-famous Sugar and Rice dance in your very own Middle School Auditorium. Who knows, they may even make you an Honorary Rice Girl!

10/1   Basketball superstar Ty Morris shows a clip from his new documentary film, How to Slam Your Way to Success, and gives advice on how to handle life as well as a crossover dribble.

Unit 5   Capitalization and Punctuation

Grade 6   Unit 5 Capitalization and Punctuation   Blackline Master 5-8

Name _____

Directions: Write definitions or rules. List pronouns. Then write sample sentences.

Pronouns

A pronoun is _____.

A subject pronoun is _____
_____
_____.

List of subject pronouns

_____ _____

_____ _____

_____ _____

Sentence _____
_____
_____

An object pronoun is _____
_____
_____.

List of object pronouns

_____ _____

_____ _____

_____ _____

Sentence _____
_____
_____

Pronouns

In Compound Subjects

Rule _____
_____

Sentence _____
_____
_____
_____

In Compound Objects

Rule _____
_____

Sentence _____
_____
_____
_____

Use with Lessons 1, 2, and 5.

Grade 6   Unit 6 Pronouns Blackline Master 6–1

6-1

Name _____   **Directions:** Write the definition. List the possessive pronouns that belong in each box and write sentences using them. Then write the rule and sample sentences in the last box.

Possessive Pronouns

A possessive pronoun shows _____.

List of possessive pronouns

_____ _____ _____ _____

_____ _____ _____ _____

_____ _____ _____ _____

Used before Nouns

_____ _____

_____ _____

_____ _____

Sentence _____

_____

_____

Used Alone

_____ _____

_____ _____

_____ _____

Sentence _____

_____

_____

Pronouns After Linking Verbs

Rule _____

_____

Sentences

1 _____

_____

2 _____

_____

Directions: Complete each definition. Fill in the list of pronouns and write sample sentences.

we and us

Use _____ with a subject.

Use _____ with a direct object.

Sentences

1 _____

_____

2 _____

_____

who, whom, whose

Use _____ as a subject pronoun.

Use _____ as a direct object pronoun.

Use _____ as a possessive pronoun.

Sentences

1 _____

_____

2 _____

_____

3 _____

_____

More Pronouns

Indefinite Pronouns

Definition: _____

_____

List of indefinite pronouns

_____   _____   _____

_____   _____   _____

Sentence

_____

_____

LESSON 1

Writing Wrap-Up: Editorial

Some students at Rice want the woods behind the school cleared for a sports field. We do need a playing field. But we also need the woods. Our nature walks there have made science come alive for all of us. It has many birds, animals, and plants. They teach us more about wild creatures than any book could do. The woods already give us a place to practice some sports. Just think of what winter recesses would be like without the pond to skate on. We could also use the trees and rocks there to set up equipment for an orienteering course. Ms. Angeli is generous to approve replacing the woods with a playing field, but what would she do without its paths to stroll in during her break? I've seen how those strolls brighten her mood on a hard day. Come to the student council meeting this Wednesday, and help us find other places to build a playing field, save the old woods, and do what is right for all members of our school community.

Unit 6 Pronouns

LESSON 2

Writing Wrap-Up: Essay

I am a white-coated, four-legged animal with fierce blue eyes and a bushy tail. I don't usually write letters, but I heard about your search for a new school symbol and decided to apply for it. I feel that my experience hunting with my pack qualifies me for the job. Perhaps the idea of a hunter doesn't appeal to you. But look at it this way. Hunters have to be very cooperative with their group. Each member of my pack is a buddy, and I do all I can to help him or her. What quality could be more important to a school than team spirit? If you want me for your school symbol, I can be reached by long howls, preferably outside the classroom.

Unit 6 Pronouns

LESSON 3

Writing Wrap-Up: Cause and Effect

Four years ago, a demolition crew knocked down the old building next to my house. At first the empty lot was ugly—just dirt, rubble, and broken boards. No plants grew there, but I saw some sparrows scratching in the dirt. That spring something interesting happened. I guess some seeds blew into the lot, or maybe the sparrows brought them, because a few plants started to grow, and ivy crept up the fences. Some wildflowers bloomed; their scent was beautiful. By the second summer, tall grasses and wildflowers covered the lot, attracting bees, grasshoppers, and several kinds of butterflies. A pair of finches built a nest in the ivy. I watched the nest for days, until finally I spotted its new occupants—three tiny, featherless chicks. By the third year, oak trees and walnut trees had taken root. This year, hummingbirds appeared when the wildflowers began to bloom. On weekends my mother and I like to eat our lunch in the empty lot, which no longer seems so empty.

Unit 6   Pronouns

LESSON 4

Writing Wrap-Up: Dialogue

Sabrina: Who do you think is the best girl dancer in class?

Jerome: Well, Suzette is the most graceful, but Judy spins better. And then Bettina gets more into the mood of the music. I'd say the best dancer is she.

Sabrina: Really? She has no sense of rhythm. Didn't you notice that the only one keeping the beat was I?

Jerome: Is that what you were doing? I thought you were playing soldier. By the way, which of us guys do you think is the best dancer?

Sabrina: Well, it isn't you.

Unit 6   Pronouns

LESSON 5

Writing Wrap-Up: Journal Entry

November 3

I would like to cook Thanksgiving dinner this year with my sister and brother. Samantha and Paolo can do the shopping, while I organize the kitchen. She knows all the best brands of spices and other gourmet items. He's good at judging a turkey and choosing the best vegetables and fruit. Maybe she and I should write out a list before they go. Paolo will try to sneak in junk food if I don't make it clear exactly what I want. He and she can carry the groceries home. Samantha and I will take charge of the cooking. It will take her and me to season things just right. She and I will also add all the garnishes. Paolo can carry the turkey to the table and carve it.

Unit 6   Pronouns

LESSON 6

Writing Wrap-Up: Survey Questions

1. About how many hours a week do you spend watching TV?
2. Who watches TV the most in your house?
3. With whom do you watch TV most often—friends, family, or your family pet?
4. Who are your favorite TV actors?
5. Which commercial do you like the least?
6. Whose opening theme song do you like the best?
7. Who limits or controls your TV watching time?
8. If you could model your life after a TV character, who would it be and why?

Unit 6   Pronouns

LESSON 7

Writing Wrap-Up: Post Card

Dear Erin,

I never thought we small town students could make it to the National Science Fair, but here we are! This morning the judges took all of us competitors around to see the science projects. There are some really great exhibits! One student built a miniature solar-powered car. Another student made a device that tells you in a squeaky voice how to schedule your life, such as when to do your homework or take the dog for a walk. We students all agreed that it would be even nicer if someone made a device that actually did the homework! Our projects look pretty impressive, too. Wouldn't it be great if one of us kids won a prize?

Love,
Patrice

LESSON 8

Writing Wrap-Up: Announcement

This Saturday afternoon at 2:00, Sweet Z will be hosting a Rap-Jams concert at Wheaton Middle School. The concert will be open to all. The tickets are $5. The proceeds from the concert will go toward building a new Wheaton music department with a hip-hop studio and rap-jam facility. Sweet Z will sign autographs for anyone who stays after the concert. If you have any questions about anything, please call or e-mail Wheaton Middle School. Come one, come all.

Name _____   **Directions:** Complete the definitions. Fill in the list of prepositions. In the last two boxes, write example sentences.

Prepositions and Prepositional Phrases

Prepositions

A preposition is _____

_____.

List of prepositions

_____ _____ _____ _____

_____ _____ _____ _____

_____ _____ _____ _____

_____ _____ _____ _____

Prepositional Phrases

A prepositional phrase is _____

_____.

Adjective Phrase

Definition: _____

_____

_____

Sentence

_____

_____

_____

Adverb Phrase

Definition: _____

_____

_____

Sentence

_____

_____

_____

Name _____   **Directions:** Fill in the definitions and write the example sentences.

Prepositions and Adverbs

Most words used as _____ can also be used as _____.

Adverb

An adverb _____

_____ .

Sentence _____

_____

_____

Preposition

A preposition _____

_____ .

Sentence _____

_____

_____

Preposition or Adverb?

Sentences (Underline the adverbs and circle the prepositions.)

1 _____

2 _____

3 _____

4 _____

Using Prepositions Correctly

The preposition *in* means _____ .

The preposition *into* means _____ .

Sentences

1 _____

2 _____

LESSON 1

Writing Wrap-Up: Scientific Observation

Over the past year, I have been watching a fig tree grow in our backyard. My father and I planted the tree last spring. During the first six months, our tree grew steadily to a height of almost five feet. A downy, greenish bark grew over the branches. Yellowish leaves, rough above and smooth beneath, began to appear. Now there are tiny yellow flowers blossoming, and my Dad says these flowers will become figs in a few weeks.

Unit 7   Prepositional Phrases

LESSON 2

Writing Wrap-Up: Review

This summer I saw two concerts in Central Park. The performers at the first concert sang old folk songs. The nicest part for me was listening to the people in the crowd singing. The songs must have brought up memories for them. I could see tears in some people's eyes. The musicians at the second concert played hip-hop music. The music was more dynamic. Everyone in this audience swayed and danced as they listened. There was even a group of kids in the front beating on drums!

Unit 7   Prepositional Phrases

LESSON 3

Writing Wrap-Up: Autobiography

(Sample Questions: What day were you born?
Where?
What is your favorite activity?)

On November 18, my mom got a big surprise. She gave birth to me on the same day on which she had been born thirty years earlier. She said she had never gotten a nicer or louder birthday present in her whole life. The rest of my life has been like the beginning—full of nice, sometimes loud surprises. I am now in the sixth grade. I started my musical career last November when I got a drum set for my birthday. My mom says the biggest surprise is that I am even louder on the drums than I was on our birthday morning twelve years ago.

Unit 7   Prepositional Phrases

LESSON 4

Writing Wrap-Up: Story

There was nothing there, only shadows. "Celia," I said, "did you hear that noise behind the curtains?" I wanted to go back down. I wanted to run down the stairs with Celia, far away from that scary room. I whirled around and looked around me. "Celia?" I could feel myself trembling. She was gone. The room was dark and quiet. Then suddenly, in a flash of light, the curtains lifted and out came all of my friends. Celia came out of the corner where she had been hiding. "Surprise," she said. "Happy thirteenth birthday!"

Unit 7   Prepositional Phrases

LESSON 5

Writing Wrap-Up: Letter

Dear Douglas,

Yesterday James and I went rowing on Carver Pond. Taking out a rowboat looks easy, but you should have seen us trying to lift that heavy boat into the water. When we were finally floating on the pond, James was so happy that he began to sing "Row, Row, Row Your Boat." He probably would have kept singing it all afternoon if it hadn't been for an accident. James stood up just as the boat went under a tree, and a low-hanging branch knocked him into the water. I jumped in with him. "What made you aim for that tree?" he asked. "Well," I told him, trying to hide a smile. "It could have had something to do with the way you were singing that song."

Your comrade,

Manuel

Unit 7   Prepositional Phrases

Here is Tony Alonso's revised working draft of his opinion essay.

Why I Love Baseball
∧ A Great Sport

To me, baseball is the best sport in the world. There are three good reasons

backing up my claim? Keep on reading to find out how baseball is the best sport in the

world.

The first reason that   is
∧ Baseball is a great sport ∧ because it has the some of the best all-around

athletes. If you've ever watched a really great championship team play, you know

what I mean. Players on these teams are some of the greatest most skilled

all-around athletes of all time. Football and soccer fans may disagree, but I think

the skills needed to be a first-rate baseball player are tougher to master than

those needed for other sports.

The second reason backing up my claim is that
∧ Playing baseball can teach you a lot about life. I can truly say that learning the

game taught me about fair play and how to listen. To be a power hitter you must

"Strike one . . . strike two . . . strike three!
You're out of here!" Are you thrilled right at this
moment? Are you in agony? It all depends. Were
you in the batter's box or in the field? Was that
hitter batting for your favorite team or against
it? Whether you're playing or watching, winning
or losing, baseball is a great sport.

run fast, hit with great power, and make
acrobatic catches. They also use game
strategy well, deciding when to hit and where to
throw the ball in only a fraction of a second.

8–1B

Here is Tony Alonso's revised working draft of his opinion essay.
(continued)

~~have a good stance, grip the bat properly, and keep your eye on the ball.~~

Last but not least is baseball's ~~Then there is the~~ fun factor. Watching a baseball game is suspenseful and exciting. Whenever I sit in the stands and watch a game, I always end up biting my nails from the tension. Who will win this one? Will my favorite team have a chance at the World Series this year? You never know which player is going to ~~hit~~ smash a homer, strike out, steal a base, or hit a foul that a fan can actually catch. One of the most ~~exciting~~ thrilling times in my life was catching a foul ball that came screaming straight for me. It ~~fell straight~~ smacked right into my outstretched hand—what a day!

As you can see, baseball truly is a great sport. In my opinion, no true sports fan can turn down a chance to see—or play in—a game. "Batter up!" Oh, the game is starting again! I've got to go. See you at the ballpark!

Our base coach is the one who helped me most with this. "Run to first!" he shouted to me during a game. I ran to third base instead and was tagged out before I even reached second base. That was my first lesson in listening to the base coach! He tells you when to go, stop, or steal. Now, of course, you don't steal in the real world; it's just a term used in baseball. However, baseball teaches you that it's hard to get away with stealing, no matter where you do it! It also teaches you how to play against a team without hating the other guys if they win instead of you.

, like seeing an action movie for the first time or watching fireworks on the Fourth of July

Name _____

Directions: This chart will help you elaborate the reasons for your opinion. Write as many details as you can to support the reasons for your opinion.

8-2

Explore Your Opinion

Opinion

Reason:	Reason:	Reason:
Details:	Details:	Details:

Name _____

Plan Your Opinion

My Opinion: _____

1. Audience

Who will read my opinion essay? Classmates? My parents? Readers of the local newspaper?

_____

_____

_____

_____

2. Reasons

Choose at least three reasons from your opinion pyramid. Reread your opinion and be sure each reason explains why you think this particular way. Now list your reasons from least to most important *and* from most to least important.

_____ _____
most important reason   least important reason

_____

_____

_____ _____
least important reason   most important reason

Which way will better help your chosen audience understand your opinion?

3. Transitional Words and Phrases

Brainstorm words and phrases you might be able to use when you organize your reasons in paragraphs and connect the paragraphs in the order of importance you have chosen.

_____

_____

_____

_____

Name _____

Evaluating Your Opinion Essay

▶ **Directions:** Reread your opinion essay. What do you need to do to make it better? Use this rubric to help you decide. Check the sentences that describe your essay.

Loud and Clear!

- ☐ The introduction will make my readers want to read on.
- ☐ My opinion is focused. I state it in one clear sentence.
- ☐ At least three specific reasons support my opinion.
- ☐ Thought-provoking details elaborate each reason.
- ☐ My reasons are in a clear order of importance.
- ☐ Engaging language expresses my thoughts and feelings.
- ☐ My conclusion wraps up my essay in an interesting way.
- ☐ *There are few mistakes in grammar, spelling, or punctuation.*

Sounding Stronger

- ☐ This introduction feels flat. It will be boring to read.
- ☐ My opinion is too broad. I need to narrow my focus.
- ☐ Some of my reasons don't support my opinion.
- ☐ Some details are too vague to explain my reasons.
- ☐ My ideas are in order but lack transitions.
- ☐ I sound confident, but some of my language is overblown.
- ☐ My conclusion just repeats everything I've already said.
- ☐ *Mistakes in grammar make my opinion confusing.*

Turn Up the Volume

- ☐ What introduction? I forgot to write one.
- ☐ I never clearly say how I think or feel.
- ☐ My reasons don't support my opinion.
- ☐ I need a lot more details to explain my reasons.
- ☐ The order of my reasons is confusing. I repeat myself.
- ☐ I can't hear myself in my writing.
- ☐ There is no conclusion. I just stopped writing.
- ☐ *Too many mistakes make the essay very hard to read.*

A Writing Conference
Opinion Essay

Have a writing conference with a partner.

If you are the listener: Use the questions below to help you think about the opinion essay.

If you are the writer: Use the questions to help you think about what to ask your listener.

Questions for the Writing Conference

- Does the introduction make you curious about the writer's opinion?

- Is the opinion supported by specific, interesting reasons?

- Is each reason elaborated with vivid details?

- Have the reasons been organized in order of importance? Would reversing the order strengthen the essay?

- Is the language expressive and engaging? Are there words that could be more precise or direct?

- Does the essay end with a final comment?

My Conference Notes

If you are the listener, make notes about what you like, what questions you have, or other suggestions. If you are the writer, make notes to remember your partner's thoughts or ideas of your own.

Here is Jessica Figueroa's revised working draft of her persuasive essay.

Music Will Amaze You!
                ∧ Music

~~I think~~ Music is a great thing! It amazes me how much music does for us. ~~Lots of kids don't realize just how important music is.~~

> I strongly believe that more kids should get involved with music.

~~You could learn more about Louis Armstrong and other musicians. It's always good to know about famous musicians. Louis Armstrong traveled all over the world performing music until he died in 1971. His nickname was "Satchmo." He recorded a lot of records and appeared in many shows.~~

Have you ever been stressed out from school? Try to listening to music. Put on your favorite CD, sit or lie down, close your eyes, and listen. Lose yourself in the music, and your stress will begin to go away. After a few minutes of listening to

> what is stressing it out

music, you'll feel better because music helps your mind let go of ~~stress.~~ Put a little rhythm into your relaxation!

> Some people think that plopping down in front of the TV is a good way to relax, but there is a better way.

> Watching TV may take no energy, but TV is way too busy to help you relax the way music can.

Name _____

Here is Jessica Figueroa's revised working draft of her persuasive essay. *(continued)*

Most important,
> Have you noticed how some music makes you feel happy and other music makes

you feel sad? The musicians who made that music were expressing their emotions

and creativity. If you play an instrument, you will also be able to express yourself in

such a way.

Also,
> Have you ever caught yourself dancing to a good song on the radio? If you're

out of shape but don't like to do sports, you can dance your way into good physical

condition! Studies show that dancing makes you stronger and more coordinated.

Certain dances even include jumping, which is a great aerobic exercise according

to the American Heart Association.

As you can see,
> Music is more than just popping a CD into your stereo. Get involved in music!

You'll be amazed too.

There are many instruments to choose from. Experiment by playing different ones or by thinking about different instruments you like to listen to. Then choose one to learn to play. I have been really happy and able to express myself since I learned to play the piano. Although it may take some time to learn to play an instrument well, in the end you will have a way to create your own beautiful music.

Just listening to music is a joy, but you can also use music to help you relax, to get exercise, and to express yourself.

Name _____

Explore Your Goal And Reasons

Directions: The diagram shown below will help you explore your goal and reasons and make sure you have enough facts or examples to support it.

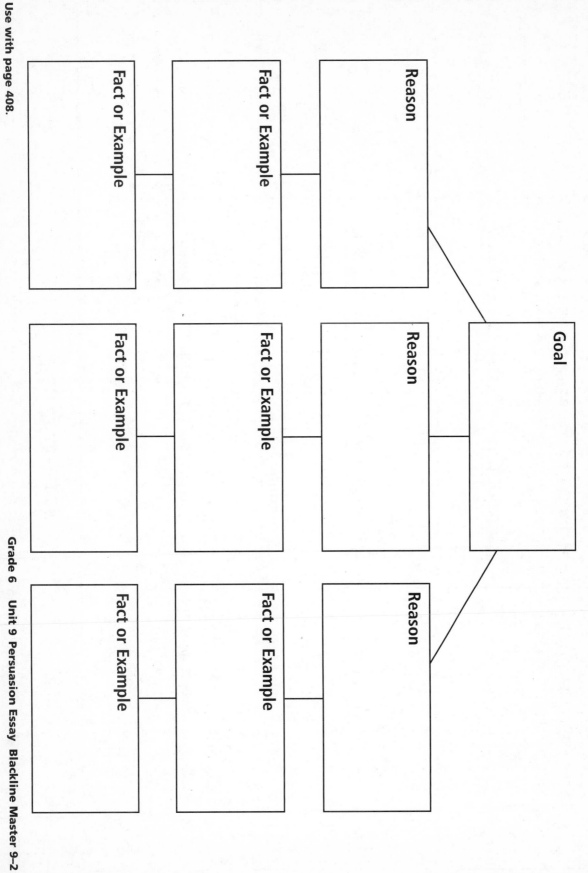

Use with page 408.

Directions: Use this chart to help you plan your persuasive essay.

Plan Your Essay

My Opinion: _____

1. Audience

Who will read my persuasive essay? Classmates? My parents? Readers of the local newspaper?

_____
_____
_____
_____
_____

2. Reasons

Review your persuasion diagram and choose at least three of the strongest reasons. Will they be convincing to your chosen audience? Now order them from least important to most important and from most important to least important.

most important reason

_____
_____
_____

least important reason

least important reason

_____
_____
_____

most important reason

Compare the results to decide which order suits your argument and will be more persuasive to your audience.

3. Objections

Write at least one objection to each reason in your argument.

_____
_____
_____

Which of the objections will be most relevant to your audience?

_____
_____
_____

Name _____

Evaluating Your
Persuasive Essay

▶ **Directions:** Reread your persuasive essay. What do you need to do to make it better? Use this rubric to help you decide. Check the sentences that describe your essay.

Loud and Clear!

☐ My introduction includes a clear statement of my goal.
☐ I have at least three strong reasons to support my goal.
☐ Facts and examples elaborate each reason.
☐ The order of my reasons makes sense.
☐ My voice sounds positive and fits my audience.
☐ I have answered possible objections.
☐ My conclusion forcefully presents my reasons and my goal.
☐ *There are few mistakes in grammar, spelling, or punctuation.*

Sounding Stronger

☐ My introduction does not clearly state my goal.
☐ I have only one or two strong reasons to support my goal.
☐ My reasons need more facts and examples.
☐ I haven't ordered my reasons carefully.
☐ My voice could fit my audience better.
☐ I mention an objection but don't answer it.
☐ My conclusion is not strong enough.
☐ *I made at least one mistake in every paragraph.*

Turn Up the Volume

☐ I never stated my goal.
☐ My reasons are unclear.
☐ Every reason needs more facts and examples.
☐ The order of my reasons is confusing.
☐ My audience might not like the way I sound.
☐ I haven't answered possible objections.
☐ My conclusion does not sum up my reasons or restate my goal.
☐ *Too many mistakes make my essay hard to understand.*

A Writing Conference
Persuasive Essay

Have a writing conference with a partner.

If you are the listener: Use the questions below to help you think about the persuasive essay.

If you are the writer: Use the questions to help you think about what to ask your listener.

Questions for the Writing Conference

- Is the goal of this persuasive essay clear?

- Is it supported by at least three strong reasons?

- Are the reasons supported by facts and examples?

- Would changing the order of the reasons strengthen the argument?

- Who is the audience? Does the essay answer objections the audience might have?

- Is the voice confident and positive and does it fit the audience?

- Does the ending restate the goal and call readers to action?

Use with page 414.

My Conference Notes

If you are the listener, make notes about what you like, what questions you have, or other suggestions. If you are the writer, make notes to remember your partner's thoughts or ideas of your own.

9-5

10-1A

Here is Kyle Colligan's revised working draft of his compare-contrast essay.

∧ My Dream Diet

~~This essay is about~~ ice cream and Mexican food ~~are~~ ∧ ∥∥ are my two favorite things

If I had my way, I would have ice cream and Mexican food every day! I would eat ice cream for breakfast, Mexican food for lunch, and both again for dinner.

They simply taste great!
to eat. ∧

Even though it does not seem like ice cream and Mexican food are alike in any way,

For instance,
they have some surprising similarities. ∧ ~~They~~ are both visually appealing. When you look down
∧
at the flavors in the cooler at your favorite ice-cream shop, you see bright colors such

fresh green guacamole, creamy white sour cream, bright orange cheddar cheese, golden yellow rice, and coffee-colored frijoles (a kind of bean).

as lemon yellow, bubble-gum pink, icy white, chocolate brown, vibrant orange, and lime

Likewise,
green. ∧ As your plate of Mexican food is set in front of you, you ~~also~~ see ~~bright colors.~~ ⌐
∧

(Move to my paragraph about differences.)

Another difference is that
∧ Mexican food can be an appetizer, a main course, or a dessert, while ice cream is only

served as a dessert. Variety is another similarity. When choosing ice cream you can pick

such as vanilla, chocolate, strawberry, rocky road, and sherbert. Similarly,
from dozens of flavors. ∧ When choosing Mexican food, you can decide among dozens of

such as tacos, nachos, tamales, enchiladas, and beef fajitas

Finally,
different dishes. (Are you feeling hungry, yet?) ∧ The atmosphere where ice-cream is sold
∧

resembles the atmosphere where Mexican food is sold. Most ice-cream shops and

Name _____

Name _____

Here is Kyle Colligan's revised working draft of his compare-contrast essay. (continued)

Both are usually colorfully decorated and have lively atmospheres. Mexican restaurants are comfortable places. Like ice-cream shops, Mexican restaurants are rarely empty, and, more often, are full of happy people! How can you be grumpy when you're licking a triple scoop of mint chocolate chip ice cream or sitting in front of a sizzling plate of chicken fajitas?

Ice cream is cold, smooth, creamy, and soothing. Mexican food is hot, crunchy, chunky, and spicy. Ice-cream is most commonly served in cups, cones, or cakes. Mexican food is most commonly served on large, hot, plates, often sizzling!

However,

Can you imagine what would happen to your ice cream if it were served this way?

Last, but not least,

As you can see, ice cream and Mexican food have some interesting similarities as well as some obvious differences. I suppose I should be glad that they're not exactly alike. If I ever get my way and can eat only ice cream and Mexican food for the rest of my life, at least I won't get bored!

The differences between ice cream and Mexican food are more obvious. For example, while

I remember having ice cream after my tonsils were removed. Ice cream made me feel so much better, but even thinking about Mexican food made my throat feel worse—ouch!

(Move sentence here about differences.)

Directions: Imagine that you have been asked to make a short film about the two subjects you are planning to compare and contrast, and that you need to explore the subjects in preparation for filming. Fill out this chart and use it to help you create a Venn diagram listing details about each of your subjects.

Explore Your Essay Idea

Movie Title	Subject 1	Subject 2
How they are alike		
Images and sounds I would like to choose to show their likenesses		
How they are different		
Images and sounds I would like to choose to show their differences		

Name _____

Directions: Identify the two subjects you want to compare and contrast. Write details that tell how the subjects are different in the outer parts of the circle. Write details that tell how the subjects are alike in the space where the circles overlap.

Explore Your Essay Idea

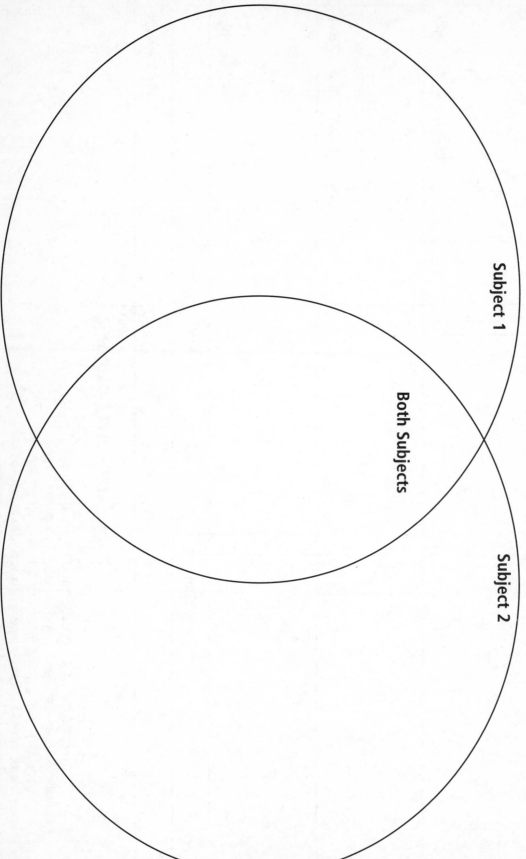

Subject 1

Both Subjects

Subject 2

Name _____ **Directions:** If you have chosen to organize your essay by similarities, then differences, use the outline on this page to help you plan it, paragraph by paragraph.

Plan Your Essay

I. Introduction

II. Similarities

    A. _____

    _____

    B. _____

    _____

    C. _____

    _____

    D. _____

    _____

III. Differences

    A. _____

    _____

    B. _____

    _____

    C. _____

    _____

    D. _____

IV. Conclusion

10–4A

Name _____   **Directions:** If you have chosen to organize your essay in feature-by-feature order, use the outline on this page to help you plan it, paragraph by paragraph.

Plan Your Essay

I. Introduction

II. Feature: _____

   A. similarities

      1. _____

      2. _____

      3. _____

   B. differences

      1. _____

      2. _____

      3. _____

III. Feature: _____

   A. similarities

      1. _____

      2. _____

      3. _____

   B. differences

      1. _____

      2. _____

      3. _____

IV. Conclusion

10–4B

Name _____

Evaluating Your
Compare-Contrast Essay

► **Directions:** Reread your essay. What do you need to do to make it better? Use this rubric to help you decide. Check the sentences that best describe your essay.

Loud and Clear!

- ☐ The introduction states my subjects and hooks my readers.
- ☐ I compare and contrast corresponding details for each subject.
- ☐ I use one method of organization throughout my essay.
- ☐ A topic sentence tells the main idea of each paragraph.
- ☐ Transitional words make similarities and differences clear.
- ☐ My conclusion sums up my ideas in a satisfying way.
- ☐ *There are few mistakes in grammar, spelling, or punctuation.*

Sounding Stronger

- ☐ The introduction states my subjects, but it's boring.
- ☐ I didn't always compare and contrast corresponding details.
- ☐ I bounce back and forth between two types of organization.
- ☐ Some paragraphs need topic sentences.
- ☐ More transitional words would sharpen the relationship between my subjects.
- ☐ My conclusion could be more memorable.
- ☐ *A number of mistakes make my essay hard to follow.*

Turn Up the Volume

- ☐ The introduction doesn't state my subjects.
- ☐ I often don't compare and contrast corresponding details about the other subject.
- ☐ I don't use either type of organization.
- ☐ None of my paragraphs have topic sentences.
- ☐ There are no transitional words.
- ☐ My essay stops short. There is no conclusion.
- ☐ *Too many mistakes make my essay hard to read.*

Name _____

A Writing Conference
Compare-Contrast Essay

Have a writing conference with a partner.

If you are the listener: Use the questions below to help you think about the compare-contrast essay.

If you are the writer: Use the questions to help you think about what to ask your listener.

Questions for the Writing Conference

- Does the introduction grab your attention? If not, could it start with a surprising fact or a question?

- Does the writer compare and contrast the same features for each subject?

- Is there one consistent method of organization?

- Would the similarities and differences be clearer if transitional words were added?

- Does each paragraph have a topic sentence that states the main idea?

- Does the conclusion sum up the main ideas in a satisfying way?

My Conference Notes

If you are the listener, make notes about what you like, what questions you have, or other suggestions. If you are the writer, make notes to remember your partner's thoughts or ideas of your own.

Name _____

11-1A

Here is Elizabeth Coultas's revised working draft of her research report.

The Duckbilled Platypus

Have you ever seen an animal that looks like a beaver and a duck all in one?

A platypus is just that! The platypus is so unusual that ~~a special scientific group~~

scientists created a special classification for this kind of mammal.

That's not so strange, but

Platypuses have thick fur that varies in color from yellowish to dark brown.

    a very   animal in other ways. This mammal   clawed

The platypus is weird-looking. ~~It~~ has a ducklike bill. It has webbed feet. It has paws.

    and   Its

with claws. It also has paddlelike limbs. It has a 14-inch barrel-shaped body. It has

ends with

a beaverlike tail. Some ~~people have even come to the conclusion that it is a crossed~~

~~animal.~~

~~A platypus is a strange sort of mammal.~~ In fact, platypuses are not cross-

breeds. ~~They have characteristics of both a mammal and a reptile.~~ They are one of

the world's two monotremes. ~~They are something like mammals and something like~~

~~reptiles, but they are actually mammals.~~ With their paddlelike limbs and their long

early scientists believed that the platypus was a cross between a mammal and a duck or reptile.

—a special class of mammals that have certain characteristics of reptiles. For example, a platypus has hair, as all mammals do. Platypus mothers feed their babies their own milk, as other mammals do. Like reptiles, however, platypus females lay leathery eggs.

Name _____

Here is Elizabeth Coultas's revised working draft of her
research report. (continued)

The only other monotreme is Australia's spiny anteater, or echidna.
tails, platypuses are also well equipped for swimming, as many reptiles are. ∧

Platypuses live in eastern Australia and Tasmania in burrows near lakes and
streams. ∧ ~~They eat many things from the lakes and streams. They have an~~

Most burrows are almost 25 feet long.

~~interesting way of getting their food.~~ When the female is ready to lay her eggs, she

makes a special burrow deep in a bank, creating an underground tunnel. She lays

from one to three eggs. Each measures about one half inch.

~~Platypuses get most of their food from the water.~~ Platypuses eat insects,

crayfish, worms, and mollusks. ∧ Platypuses cannot see when underwater, ~~their~~

from lakes and streams   because folds of skin cover their eyes, but

wide tails help them swim, and their ducklike bills help them gather their food. They

usually feed during the early morning or the late evening. The mud and sand that

platypuses end up eating along with their food help them break up their food.

Platypuses don't have teeth. ~~I think it would be fun to swim with a platypus.~~

11–1C

Here is Elizabeth Coultas's revised working draft of her research report. *(continued)*

Platypuses are now protected by law.

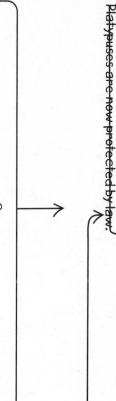

Platypuses are nearly unique animals that have adapted well to their surroundings. Although the creatures no longer baffle scientists, the study of the duckbilled platypus will surely continue for years to come.

Sources

Katz, Barbara. "Platypus." Compton's Encyclopedia Online. vers. 3.0. 1998. The Learning Company. America Online. 3 Oct. 2001.

"Platypus." National Geographic Book of Mammals. Vol. 2. Washington, DC: National Geographic, 1998.

Reilly, Pauline, and Will Rolland (illus.). Platypus. Kenthurst, Australia: Kangaroo Press, 1991.

Short, Joan, with Jack Green, Bettina Bird, and Andrew Wichlinski (illus.). Platypus. Greenvale, NY: Mondo Publishing, 1997.

Name _____

Directions: Use this chart to explore your topic.

Explore Your Topic

Topic _____

What I **K**now	What I **W**ant To Learn	Possible **S**ources

Directions: With a partner, practice distinguishing fact from
opinion by filling in this Fact and Opinion chart
about a favorite movie, book, or animal.

11-3

Research Your Topic

Topic _____

Fact	Source of Proof	Opinion

Directions: Use this blank outline to help organize your report.

Plan Your Report

Decide how you will order your main topics—from most to least important, most familiar to least familiar, in time order, by cause and effect, or another order.

If you have fewer main topics or subtopics than are shown on this outline, leave some of the spaces blank. If you have more subtopics or details, add letters or numbers and write in the margins.

I. _____

  A. _____

    1. _____

    2. _____

  B. _____

    1. _____

    2. _____

  C. _____

    1. _____

    2. _____

II. _____

  A. _____

    1. _____

    2. _____

  B. _____

    1. _____

    2. _____

  C. _____

    1. _____

    2. _____

11–4

Name _____

Evaluating Your Research Report

▶ **Directions:** Reread your report. Use this rubric to help you revise. Check the sentences that describe your report.

Loud and Clear!

- ☐ The report shows good research based on reliable sources.
- ☐ The introduction and conclusion present the main idea.
- ☐ The report is well organized. Smooth transitions connect ideas.
- ☐ Each paragraph has a topic sentence and supporting details.
- ☐ I have written in the third person and in my own words.
- ☐ My list of sources is accurate and complete.
- ☐ *There are very few spelling or grammar mistakes.*

Sounding Stronger

- ☐ Parts of the report are well researched, but others aren't.
- ☐ The introduction and conclusion are boring.
- ☐ I ordered the paragraphs well, but I need better transitions.
- ☐ Some paragraphs need topic sentences or more details.
- ☐ I give an opinion that should be deleted.
- ☐ I need to make sure that a quotation is written correctly.
- ☐ I have a list of sources, but it is incomplete.
- ☐ *Mistakes make some sentences confusing.*

Turn Up the Volume

- ☐ I have not done enough research.
- ☐ The report lacks an introduction and a conclusion.
- ☐ The paragraphs are not in an order that makes sense.
- ☐ I have few topic sentences and few supporting facts.
- ☐ The writing mixes opinions with facts.
- ☐ I have not quoted carefully. I may have plagiarized.
- ☐ I forgot to include a list of sources.
- ☐ *Mistakes make the report hard to understand.*

A Writing Conference
Research Report

Have a writing conference with a partner.

If you are the listener: Use the questions below to help you think about the research report.

If you are the writer: Use the questions to help you think about what to ask your listener.

Questions for the Writing Conference

• Does the introduction grab your attention? If not, could it begin with a surprising fact or a question?

• Is each paragraph supported by at least two facts or examples?

• Could the ideas be in a better order? Do smooth transitions connect the ideas?

• Is the report written in the third person, presenting facts and not opinions?

• Are quotations used correctly?

• Does the conclusion sum up the main idea?

• Is the list of sources in the correct format? Do the sources appear to be reliable?

My Conference Notes

If you are the listener, make notes about what you like, what questions you have, or other suggestions. If you are the writer, make notes to remember your partner's thoughts or ideas of your own.

Name _____

Completing a Form

APPLICATION
Savings Account

Please print the following information and complete all of the sections. Sign and date this application and return it to a bank representative.

Name: _____   Telephone: _____

Street: _____

City: _____   State: _____   Zip: _____

Date of Birth: _____   Occupation: _____

Mother's Maiden Name: _____

Type of Savings Account (check one):   ____ Basic   ____ MultiService

ATM Card (check one):   ____ Yes   ____ No

I certify that the information given above is accurate and correct to the best of my knowledge.

_____   _____

Signature of Applicant   Date

_____   _____

Signature of Parent/Guardian   Date

Signature of parent or guardian required if applicant is under 18 years of age.

Name _____

Directions: Feedback is useful for improving a speaker's performance during an oral presentation. Evaluate your own oral reports or the classroom presentations given by others.

Oral Presentation Rating Sheet

Effective Use of Voice

Rate the presentation based on the speaker's delivery. Give specific comments on how improvements can be made.

	Acceptable	Needs Improvement
Volume, or loudness of voice		
Pitch (high or low)		
Stress (emphasis on words)		
Pace, or rate of speaking		
Pronunciation		

Effective Use of Media

Rate the presentation based on the speaker's use of visual aids or media aids. Give specific comments on how improvements can be made.

Aids were . . .	Acceptable	Needs Improvement
prepared and set up in advance		
easy to see or hear		
helpful for understanding the topic		
simple, clear, free of errors		
presented well by the speaker		

Name _____

Here is Ray Kramka's revised working draft of his personal narrative.

> B.R. (Bored Room)
> ^ Waiting Room

It started on a nice sunny day—birds were chirping, dogs were barking, and I

was yelling, "Ouch!" Out in the backyard I was playing with my dog, Clancy. I was

~~falling over because of that crazy dog. When he plays outdoors, he really gets~~

~~excited. Usually that's fun, but he doesn't know his own strength. That's Clancy for~~

~~you.~~ I was about to throw a tennis ball for him to fetch when he jumped on me,

knocking me into a hole where there used to be a well.

> rocks, dirt, leaves, twigs, and a tree stump
> The old well was filled with ~~stuff.~~ ^ My arm landed right on the stump, and my

body landed on top of my arm. It didn't hurt too much until I turned over to get up.

cold and numb, and I knew right away that something was broken

My right elbow felt ~~weird.~~ ^

My mom was at work when this happened, so I asked a neighbor to call her at

work. ~~When she got in her car to drive home, the battery was dead because she~~

12-1A

Name _____

Here is Ray Kramka's revised working draft of his personal narrative. (continued)

had left the lights on. Then she had to borrow someone else's car.

As soon as my mom got home, I jumped in the car. She helped me put on my

seatbelt because I could barely move my arm. While she was buckling the seatbelt,

her purse hit the button, making the seatbelt snap back against my arm. Ouch! She

felt really bad about that. She apologized to me. On the way, we had to pick up my

sister at aftercare. My sister was really disappointed to leave because she was the

caller for bingo that day.

When we finally got to the emergency room, we sat in the waiting room for

thirty minutes. Then a nurse showed us to a room with a table, and I got to lie down

on it. She asked if we wanted to watch a movie while we were waiting for a doctor.

The choices were Barney, Lamb Chop's Play Along, and Sesame Street. We said,

"No, thanks."

We waited in the room for about two and a half hours.
After a while,
We were so bored, we

wished we were watching Barney.
Sometime during the long wait,
My mom saw red dots appearing on my face.

12–1C

Here is Ray Kramka's revised working draft of his personal narrative. (continued)

                                                        Soon
^They were on my stomach, in my hair, and my arms too. "Oh, no!" I thought, but I
                              my scalp

didn't say anything. A doctor came in. My mom asked him if the dots on my head
                                                                                        I felt a bit scared and worried that my body
                                                                                        was falling apart on me. When a doctor finally
were chicken pox. He said yes. ¶ He said that I was going to the x-ray room. He   came, my mom asked, "Are the dots on Roy's
                                                                                        head chicken pox?"

seemed to be in a big hurry.
                                                                                        He answered, "Yes! That certainly does look like
                                                                                        chicken pox." Then
A few minutes later, a nurse walked in with a wheelchair and one of those

masks doctors use in the E.R. When I finally got to the x-ray room, I had to put my

arm between two pieces of metal so they could take pictures of it. I had to put on

the mask and be rolled to the x-ray room in the wheelchair. Rolling down the hall

was probably the worst part of my grand adventure. It was hard to breathe through

the mask, and it smelled like stuff you clean with ammonia.

           The x-ray technician bent my arm back until I thought it would snap. Ouch!
                                                                                        "You have a hairline fracture in your elbow," he
After I got back to the E.R., the same doctor came in to tell us my arm was broken.   said. Then he added, "But a cast won't help in
                                                                                        the part of your arm that was hurt.
He said I had a hairline fracture in my elbow, but a cast wouldn't help in the part of ¶

Here is Ray Kramka's revised working draft of his
personal narrative. (continued)

~~my arm that was hurt.~~ ~~He also said~~ it wouldn't be fun anyway to have chicken pox

under a cast. He put my arm in a sling and said we could go home. When we left the

                                    made
hospital, it was around 11:30 P.M. We just ~~had~~ one more stop, the pharmacy, to pick

up a prescription for pain medicine. We got home after midnight.

              By the time   , it had been over twelve hours since I had fallen into the hole

Do good things come to those who wait?
Just getting home was good enough for me.
I felt relieved! Now I just had to wait out
the chicken pox.

Name _____

Directions: Use this memory chart to explore your topic. Under each heading, note what you remember about your story idea. Don't worry about making errors.

Explore Your Story Idea

Events	People

Places	Objects

Name _____   **Directions:** Use this blank story narrative to plan your personal narrative.

Plan Your Narrative

Reread your memory chart. Then fill in the outline with the main events in time order. Finally, write related details, taking some from your memory chart and adding any others.

1. _____

    Detail: _____

    Detail: _____

    Detail: _____

    Detail: _____

2. _____

    Detail: _____

    Detail: _____

    Detail: _____

    Detail: _____

3. _____

    Detail: _____

    Detail: _____

    Detail: _____

    Detail: _____

4. _____

    Detail: _____

    Detail: _____

    Detail: _____

    Detail: _____

12–3

Name _____

Evaluating Your Personal Narrative

▶ **Directions:** Reread your narrative. How can you improve it? Use this rubric to help you decide. Check the sentences that describe your narrative.

Loud and Clear!

☐ I grab my readers' attention right away.
☐ I present the main events in order, using time-clue words.
☐ Interesting details make my story come alive.
☐ My personal voice carries through from start to finish.
☐ The strong ending tells a feeling, shows an action, or finishes in another way.
☐ *I have made very few grammar or spelling mistakes.*

Sounding Stronger

☐ My beginning needs more pizzazz.
☐ Some events are not in order. I need more time-clue words.
☐ I have too many details about unimportant things.
☐ I need more details about important things.
☐ My voice is clear in some places, but not everywhere.
☐ My ending is not strong enough.
☐ *My mistakes sometimes get in the way of telling the story.*

Turn Up the Volume

☐ My beginning is just too dull.
☐ The order of events is confusing.
☐ The action, the people, and the setting need details.
☐ My voice is flat. I don't sound like the person I am.
☐ I really don't have an ending yet.
☐ *Lots of mistakes make the narrative hard to read.*

A Writing Conference
Personal Narrative

Have a writing conference with a partner.

If you are the listener: Use the questions below to help you think about the personal narrative.

If you are the writer: Use the questions to help you think about what to ask your listener.

Questions for the Writing Conference

- Does the introduction grab your attention? Would it be improved if it started with some dialogue, a description, or a teaser?

- Does the writer use the pronoun *I*?

- Have events been presented in the order in which they happened? Are there enough time order words?

- Does the narrative need more details about what the writer heard, tasted, smelled, saw, or felt?

- Does the writer's personality come through?

- Is the ending satisfying? Does it tell what the writer felt or show an action?

My Conference Notes

If you are the listener, make notes about what you like, what questions you have, or other suggestions. If you are the writer, make notes to remember your partner's thoughts or ideas of your own.

13–1A

Here is Dava Hollingsworth's revised working draft of her story.

Invasion!
~~Maggie's Birthday~~

Imaginary space creatures were ~~Maggie's~~ the hobby, and she knew all about them.
(her)

It was Maggie's birthday, and she couldn't wait to see what the day had in store for her. She was sitting next to her computer in her bedroom, reading her newest comic book, *Invaders from Outer Space.*

Suddenly, without warning, her the computer flickered on all by itself.

"What's going on?" Maggie shouted. She was so startled, she jumped up and ran

away from it. Then, just as suddenly, she felt herself begin moving toward the

screen. It was almost as if a force were drawing her near.

The computer screen changed from bright green to bright purple. This

frightened Maggie because her monitor had always been black and white. As

Maggie stood there staring at the bright purple screen, a strange face appeared.

"Who are you?" whispered Maggie, as if the face could hear her. It looked like the

space creature in her comic book!

The face was silver, as though made entirely out of metal, and it had huge, saucer-shaped black eyes. The eyes never blinked. They just kept staring straight at her.

Name _____

Here is Dava Hollingsworth's revised working draft of her story.
(continued)

Frantically,
      "Hello? Is anyone here? Where is everybody?"
Maggie began searching the house, but she could find no one. Her heart was ∧

pounding harder and harder. All she could think about was that strange face on her

computer monitor. Her family wouldn't have left her alone, not on her birthday.

Could they have seen the space creatures and run out? Could the space creatures

be in the house even now?

    Suddenly Maggie saw movement all around her. She screamed, sure that the

creatures had found her.

    "Surprise! Happy birthday, Maggie!" Everyone was yelling at once as they jumped

out of their hiding places.

    Maggie's father smiled and said, "We meant to surprise you for your birthday,
                     gently ∧
Maggie, not scare you to death. Are you okay?"

    Maggie told her father about the space creature on the computer screen. She
~~talked really fast. She told him the whole family had to get out of the house.~~

"Dad, there's something wrong with my computer!" Maggie said breathlessly. "It came on all by itself!" The words came tumbling out as fast as she could say them. "And the screen turned purple! I saw a space creature on the screen! We've got to get out of here! Quickly!"

Name _____

Here is Dava Hollingsworth's revised working draft of her story.
(continued)

firmly
"Maggie, calm down," replied her father ⋏. "That's not your old computer. It looks

the same, but we wanted to surprise you with a color monitor for your birthday. I set

a timer so it would come on while we were hiding. That 'space creature' you saw on

the monitor is your new screen saver!"

After she had calmed down a bit, Maggie sat down with her family to open the

rest of her presents.

> One box was wrapped in blue paper with a shiny
> purple ribbon. As Maggie began to untie the ribbon,
> the box popped open! Maggie screamed again. It
> was a toy space creature!

> "This has certainly been a day full of excitement,"
> said Maggie's mother.
> "Maybe too exciting!" Maggie said with a grin. "I
> thought I was a goner! I know I've read enough space
> creature comic books for a while!"

Name _____   **Directions:** This chart will help you explore the main characters in your story. Fill out a chart for each main character.

Explore Your Characters and Setting

Fill in the names and details about the characters. These questions are examples; add questions that are better suited to your characters.

Name of Character _____

Think About . . .	Ask Yourself . . .	Answers
Appearance	Does this character wear a hat? Have red hair? Run like a stampeding horse? _____ _____ _____	
Actions	Does this character eat chili for breakfast? Ride a skateboard to school? Hand in homework early? _____ _____ _____	
Thoughts or feelings	Is this character nervous about school? Happy alone in the woods at night? Sad because a relative died? _____ _____ _____	
Interests	Does this character scuba dive? Play chess? Sing in a band? _____ _____ _____	

13-2

Directions: Use this chart to help develop the setting for your story. List specific details about where and when the story happens.

Explore Your Characters and Setting

Think About . . .	Ask Yourself . . .	Details
Place	Where does the story take place? On a clipper ship or a space ship? In my living room or an ancient castle?	
Time	When does my story happen? A thousand years from now or the day after tomorrow?	

Name _____

Explore and Plan Your Story

Directions: Use this story map to plan the beginning, middle, and end of your story.

13–4

Beginning
Tell important details about characters and setting, and introduce the conflict.

↓

Middle
Show the characters trying to deal with the conflict.

↓

End
Show how the conflict is resolved.

Evaluating Your Story

► **Directions:** Reread your story. What do you need to do to make it better? Use this rubric to help you decide. Check the sentences that describe your narrative.

Loud and Clear!

- ☐ Dialogue makes my characters seem real.
- ☐ Details show when and where the story takes place.
- ☐ The plot has a conflict, a climax, and a resolution.
- ☐ My language creates a definite mood that suits my story.
- ☐ I chose one point of view and stayed with it.
- ☐ The opening introduces my characters and setting.
- ☐ The ending shows how the conflict is resolved.
- ☐ *There are very few mistakes in grammar, spelling, or punctuation.*

Sounding Stronger

- ☐ I need more dialogue to show how my characters think and feel.
- ☐ Specific details would make the setting clearer.
- ☐ Some events are unrelated to the conflict.
- ☐ My voice is not strong, and so the mood is not clear.
- ☐ I change point of view once or twice.
- ☐ My beginning introduces setting and characters but could be more interesting. The ending is too abrupt.
- ☐ *Mistakes sometimes make the story hard to read.*

Turn Up the Volume

- ☐ The characters don't seem real. There isn't any dialogue.
- ☐ My story has no clear setting.
- ☐ What's the conflict? Many events are unnecessary.
- ☐ The story has no emotional effect at all.
- ☐ The point of view wanders, making the story hard to follow.
- ☐ The beginning is confusing. It's not clear what happens at the end.
- ☐ *Many mistakes make the story very difficult to read.*

A Writing Conference
Story

Have a writing conference with a partner.

If you are the listener: Use the questions below to help you think about the story.

If you are the writer: Use the questions to help you think about what to ask your listener.

Questions for the Writing Conference

- Are the characters interesting and believable? Does dialogue show how they think, act, and feel?

- Is it clear when and where the story takes place?

- Is there an engaging plot that includes a conflict and resolution, as well as a climax?

- Are events told in order, with a clear beginning, middle, and end?

- Does the writer stick with one point of view?

- Does the opening introduce the characters and setting? Does the ending resolve the conflict?

My Conference Notes

If you are the listener, make notes about what you like, what questions you have, or other suggestions. If you are the writer, make notes to remember your partner's thoughts or ideas of your own.